Originally published as *De bakker* in Belgium
and the Netherlands by Clavis Uitgeverij, 2009
English translation from the Dutch by Clavis Publishing Inc., New York

Visit us on the Web at www.clavis-publishing.com.

Bakers and What They Do written and illustrated by Liesbet Slegers

ISBN 978-1-60537-576-2

This book was printed in June 2020 at Nikara, M. R. Štefánika 858/25, 963 01 Krupina, Slovakia.

First Edition
10 9 8 7 6 5 4 3 2 1

Clavis Publishing supports the First Amendment and celebrates the right to read.

Bakers
and What They Do

Liesbet Slegers

Clavis

NEW YORK

Mmmm! A fresh slice of bread tastes so good.

Everything from a bakery is delicious.

Rolls, croissants, cakes, pastries, cookies, pies.

Who makes these yummy treats? A baker.

Baking can be a messy job, so bakers wear
clothes that can be washed easily.
Most bakers wear white shirts and aprons.
And some bakers wear a white hat.
This baker wears special checked pants.

baker's hat

white shirt

apron

checked pants

white shoes

dough mixer

The baker needs many different tools and ingredients for his work.

For breads he uses flour, yeast, salt, and water.

Sweet treats need sugar and sometimes chocolate.

The baker uses a rolling pin to roll out pastry,

and baking pans and tins for cakes.

He uses oven mitts to take the hot loaves of bread

and cakes out of the oven.

flour

milk

yeast

salt

sugar

water

butter

cake tins

rolling pin

chocolate mold

brush

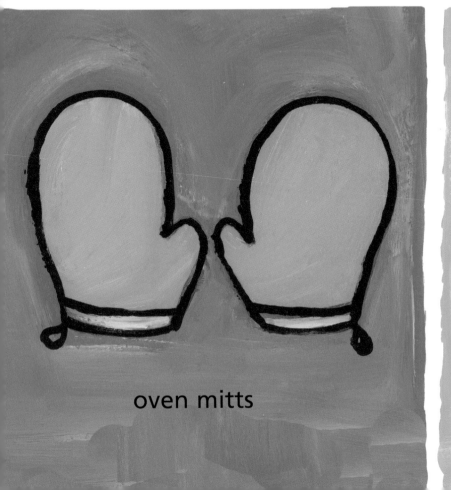

oven mitts

oven

The baker wakes up in the middle of the night to start his day.
The bread must be ready when the customers come to
the bakery in the morning.

First, a quick cup of coffee, then off to work.

Maybe he will eat some of his delicious bread for breakfast later.

The baker weighs and measures the flour.

He wants to use just the right amount.

Then the baker adds water, salt, and yeast to the bowl.

The mixer turns it into a nice, smooth dough.

Next, the baker puts a towel over the dough
and lets it rest for a while.

The yeast makes it rise and get bigger.

Now it's time to knead the dough.

The baker divides the dough into several pieces.

He rolls and punches the dough and rolls it again.

It's hard work!

Finally he puts each piece in a tin and lets it rest again.

When the dough has risen again, it's ready for the oven.
The baker puts the tins in the oven and sets a timer.

Ding!

The loaves of bread are ready.

The baker may use oven mitts or a paddle to take the hot loaves out of the oven.

Mmmm. They smell delicious!

While the bread cools, it's time to start working on some pastries.
A baker might make cakes, croissants, cookies, tarts, and more!
He uses fruit, chocolate, spices, frosting, and other goodies.
Today the baker is icing a birthday cake!

All of this happens before the bakery opens for the day.

The baker continues to work while the shopkeeper

waits on the customers.

Here comes a customer to buy a fresh loaf of bread.

"And maybe I'll take a croissant, too," she says.

"Enjoy it, and see you tomorrow!"